The Tools, The Paper & The Urge To Write

by

Goff Todd

ISBN: 978-1-910205-46-4

First published in 2015 by
For The Right Reasons
(Charity no. SC037781)
Printers & Publishers
60 Grant Street, Inverness

British Library Cataloguing in Publication Data.
A catalogue record of this book is available
from the British Library.

Contents

A letter to David   5

24 HOURS   10

Travelling   (2001)   19

Goff takes Giles canoeing
on a historic river   27

Home Waters - Getting to Know Joe   31

Aberfan   41

Some Bird   46

A Leap of Faith   48

DAD   54

Those were the Notes C. C. B. B A.A   62

The Power, and Knock-on Effect
 of Good Feedback   68

A letter to David

If I tell you that I've never written about this before, I would hate for you to read too much into that. It's not a case of my never wanting to talk about the incident, as though it equated with the horrific experiences that World War 1 veterans went through. On the other hand I suspect that in the first years after I left the Marines I did underplay the effect of it on me, and if I found myself dwelling on it, I suppose I berated myself a little for being a bit of a self indulgent wimp.

The truth is that, as I have got older, the experience has become more real and has never completely faded into the background, and I have become more willing to accept that it did have a significant emotional impact on me, and that, in part, it explains the rage and unprovoked anger that I have sometimes experienced but usually managed to contain. It was never diagnosed as *post traumatic stress,* but that is exactly what it was.

Last Spring, Terry and I went across to Dingwall to do some shopping. As we entered the car park there was an identically coloured Honda model to ours already there. As we locked our vehicle the male driver approached it, and I thought to have a chat with him about the coincidence, but, by the time we were close enough, he was already in the driver's seat and the opportunity was gone but then I spotted a small stick-on logo on the rear window, *once a Marine, always a Marine,* and that proved too much of a coincidence, so I tapped on his window.

It transpired that he was ex-45 Commando, only about 10 years younger than me, so we enjoyed a few minutes of reminiscence. But then he mentioned a name that I knew well.

'Did you know Roy Pennington?' he asked. Roy was alongside me when I got shot, one of the four of us lying on that exposed volcanic hillside but, rather than answer his question directly, I asked a question in return, 'Did he talk about Aden much?'

'All the time,' came the reply, 'always on about being shot at, and the bloke alongside him whose binoculars saved his life!'

Since that conversation in a car park I have thought about the whole experience almost on a daily basis, but I am still not sure I have it in context. I was watching the news this evening and saw the return of 40 Commando from Afghanistan and the emotional reunions the guys went through with their families, and it brought tears to my eyes. I recalled a TV programme made five years after the Falklands War, and how so many of the Marines had suffered failed marriages after their return. It is a fact that more Falklands veterans have committed suicide than were actually killed in that mini war.

I know I have often talked with you about the unifying effect of a *shared experience,* and there is nothing more extreme than active service. It is impossible to put into words the effect it can have on you, no matter how good you are at communicating. The only ones who understand are those who were there with you. Boxing is perhaps the best sporting analogy. So if it has a traumatic effect there is a limit to how many times you can talk to anyone about it, even if it is a loved one. In the end you internalise all the feelings.

On my first tour in Aden with 45 Commando in 1964 one of the lads in my section got shot. His name was Dickie Hyde and he was just 20 years old. His job? He was i/c the machine gun that was carried and fired by Norman Goode, also 20 years old. How did Dickie die? He ran just 2 metres too far in front of the machine gun as we advanced and, as Norman lifted the gun, the butt banged on the ground and this loosed off a round. The bullet took Dickie in the left buttock, but when we examined him and dressed the entry hole there was no obvious exit wound. We were young, and had no first-hand experience of death, so it didn't occur to any of us that Dickie was in mortal danger. Even he treated it almost as if it was just part of a training experience, lying there and joking with me about how he'd always wondered what it would be like to be shot. But die he did, for the bullet had ricocheted off his pelvic bone up into the chest cavity and pierced his heart, so he bled to death internally whilst on the helicopter.

Dickie was buried in the military cemetery in Aden for, in those days, bodies were not *cas-e-vaced* back to the UK. It always seemed so utterly pointless, and I often thought of his parents and how they must have grieved. You can imagine it now that you have family. I have no idea how Norman coped with it, but it must have changed him, like a malignant cancer inside eating away at you.

Anyway, I thought it was time for me to put down on paper what happened during that fateful 24 hours in '67. Goodness knows how long this will take me, but hopefully I have plenty of time!

24 Hours

We were living in what had previously been Army and Air Force Married Quarters, a multi storied housing block at the western end of Maa'lla Main Street near Steamer Point in urban Aden. All the personnel who had lived there had long since been evacuated back to the UK, and 45 Commando was charged with covering the final withdrawal of the British from the colony. 'We' consisted of elements of Support Company and all of Recce Troop; one officer, Lieutenant Terry Knott; a wonderful sergeant, Jock Strathdee, and a couple of corporals including me, and several marines, including your uncle Peter who, at 19 years old was the youngest in the troop. Our role was urban reconnaissance and instant response. The 'enemy'? Two loose knit groups of civilians, one the NLF (National Liberation Front) and the other, FLOSY (Freedom and Liberation of South Yemen), typically like the IRA and its offshoots.

Saturday, 4th November 1967

As the day progressed tensions seemed to escalate by the hour. There was a mortar bomb attack on our building, and then two shootings in the road immediately adjacent to our block. A rather stupid RAF officer was shot at as he drove past our position in his open topped sports car, and he drew a revolver and brandished it. This action almost got him shot by mistake by the Marine sentry, for we were all fairly trigger happy that day. We were called to an early evening operations briefing where Terry Knott gave us an update on the local situation, with the additional information that a large cache of weapons was suspected of being stored in a house in the nearby Arab quarter. Recce troop had been tasked with confirming this and so four of us were to head out after dark to learn what we could.

At 1900 hours Terry, Roy, Jock Strathdee and I moved out, carrying weapons, but with minimal ammunition. Recce troop was never expected to get involved in a firefight, so instead of 120 rounds of ammo, we had no more than 30 or 40 rounds each, a lot of it being tracer that we used to direct others to a target. We spent most of the night on the top of a huge oil storage tank just a few hundred yards from the house. That was eerie, as every so often the tank emitted a tremendous echoing noise as the metal contracted in the cool of the night.

Sunday 5th November

An hour before first light we moved off the tank and eased our way up the volcanic hillside until we were looking down on the houses about 400 metres below. There was no vegetation and we took up position on a small rocky ridge, using small rocks and our equipment to break up the line of our silhouettes. As the day dawned we were able to confirm that on the flat rooftop of the suspicious house there was indeed a huge cache of weapons and ammunition.

At that point we should have withdrawn, for our job was done. However, the political situation in the region was so fraught by this stage of the British withdrawal from the Protectorate, that we had a good idea that, when reported to the appropriate authorities, nothing at all would happen.

So, as the senior person present, Terry suggested that the best way of dealing with this illicit arsenal was to destroy it ourselves, and we were happy to agree. So we loaded up with tracer, used some of our water to damp down the dust in front of our rifles, and some 15 or 20 minutes before 0800 hours we opened fire.

The Arab males who were on the roof drinking tea were not really our target, but of course if you put a weapon in the hands of a human there is always a desire to kill, and so these guys were lucky to escape the initial onslaught. Within minutes the building was ablaze, but now we didn't have it all our own way, for they were shooting back at us. Even now we still had a chance to withdraw, but we didn't, and the firefight went on and on. Some 30 minutes later the local fire engine drove up the road, but we certainly didn't want the fire extinguished, so we put several rounds into the engine itself and it rapidly went into reverse and retreated.

After an hour or so our situation was getting critical, for our ammunition was almost gone and the enemy fire was becoming increasingly accurate, forcing us to keep our heads down. I was on the right of the group, and was in the prime position to see one of the Arabs break out of the house, rifle in hand, and run for the adjacent building. I missed with a couple of shots, then exchanged my rifle for my binoculars, as the long two storey white building had more than a dozen windows, and it was obvious that the Arab had moved into it to improve his angle of shooting. We had been taught to use binoculars by holding them with just thumb and forefinger, using the remaining fingers to shield the lens from reflecting light. Holding them like that and lying on my stomach I started checking each window in turn looking for movement.

The impact can only be described as immense, huge. It was like being hit in the head by a train. There was no noise, nothing apart from the immensity of the impact. I was hurled backwards in a half somersault, and, after a second or so, my brain clicked in and I knew that I had been shot and that, since it was a head shot, it followed that I must be dying. The first voice I heard was that of Roy Pennington, 'Christ! Who's that fuckin' screaming?' It was only then I realised it was me and that I was still alive. I tried to open my eyes but they wouldn't work properly. Through my slitted left eye I glimpsed my hands, for I had instinctively curled up into the foetal crouch. Both my thumbs were a mess, blood and bone, and the tip of my right index finger seemed to be missing as well.

We all carried morphine in a small ampule taped to our dog tags around our neck, and either Jock or Terry injected my dose into my arm. Shortly afterwards, the same Arab smacked a bullet through Jock's water bottle that was alongside his head, and Roy's rifle took a direct hit as he was sighting up for a shot. For the next hour I just lay there, and because I was blinded I felt terribly vulnerable, although the drug soon got into my system and made me a bit drowsy. It was only when the guys finally got to move me out that they found the binoculars, realised they had taken the full force of the bullet, and brought them out with me.

I don't recall the evacuation or arriving at the RAF hospital, and my first waking moments in late afternoon allowed me to overhear a conversation between people who I couldn't see, as my eyes and head were heavily bandaged. It was the surgeon and the Colonel of 45 Cdo, and the latter had just asked

13

whether my sight was permanently damaged. The reply amazed me for I think I was convinced it was, but he said the damage was all to the circumference of the eye sockets with over twenty stitches to the right side and seven or eight on the left. The top half of my face remained numb for months and I can still recall feeling the pins and needles that signified it returning to normal in mid March '68.

The surgery to my fingers wasn't done until the Wednesday and took place on board the commando carrier. It was the fingers that gave me the most pain, constant and almost unbearable for weeks. Just seven days after the shooting I was on my way home on a *casevac* flight. We landed in Bahrain and spent the night there, all the casualties in the RAF hospital. One of the male nurses on the ward was obviously gay (not a word we knew in '67), a 'condition' that did not officially exist in the Armed Forces, making it difficult to be around them, and so I ignored him.

My fingers were giving me a great deal of pain and it must have been etched on my face for he came across and read my medical notes. He asked what was causing the pain and then enquired as to when I had last had a shower and, when I said it was over a week, he dressed my hands in plastic bags and despatched me to the showers, saying he would renew the bandages on my hands afterwards. It was great as you can imagine, but even the lovely experience of standing under warm running water was nothing in comparison to having my fingers cleaned and dressed. He was wonderful at his job and his skill and empathy brought me great relief – if he hadn't been gay I'd have kissed him!

One of the endearing and amusing things I never forgot was the reaction of my mother to my injury. In those days if someone was killed or injured, all the Corps did was ring the nearest police station, and a constable was despatched to break the bad news. Aden is a few hours ahead of GMT, so by the time the message got through to Barry it was still before 0900 hours. My father was in church, so my mother answered the door, to be confronted by a uniformed policeman. 'Does Godfrey Todd live here?' he asked, to which Mum replied, "Yes, but it couldn't have been him as he's abroad,' a reaction that gives a clue to the worries this particular teenager put his parents through.

Copy of hand written letter from Lt. Col. J. Owen, OBE; R.M. to my parents.

Dear Mr Todd,

You will have heard by now that your son was wounded yesterday in action against the terrorists in the Ma'alla district of Aden. He was one of a small party of four on forward reconnaissance work overlooking a terrorist area when their post came under sustained fire. After a prolonged fight one of the terrorists hit the binoculars that Goff was using, the bullet passing down the right lens, shattering the prism, but missing Goff. He was very, very fortunate, but naturally his face was cut by the force of the bullet, and his fingers were cut by the fragments.

I am told by the RAF hospital that Goff was attended by a plastic surgeon, and all being well, any scars that remain will not be unsightly.

There is no doubt that Goff did well whilst in the O.P. and was a credit to you, himself, and us all.

Yours sincerely,

Lt. Col. J. Owen.

Ode to Todd-The Bread

Remember remember the 5th of November
When Wales manned an O.P. in Crater
Whilst bullets flew round, Todd stood his ground –
Like Nelson he stood – never traitor.

For an hour he fought. Of iron he was wrought,
The brave and gallant expender,
When the battle was done, 'neath Aden's
hot sun Lay the dead and a battered fire-tender!

On the ground Todd lay spent, his binoculars bent,
Surrounded by peaks tall and stark,
His unconscious mind dreamed (least that's how it seemed)
Of tries scored in Cardiff Arms Park!

Our hero's now mended, the nightmares are ended,
No more Aden and no more tight fixes;
Just war stories unending – so sad, so heartrending,
But for Bino's – those damned 126's!

(Based on Charge of the Light Brigade by Tennyson)

This 'poem' was penned by a good 'oppo' of mine, Frank Allen,
a guy from Guernsey with whom I trained and ran with for several years

Travelling 2001

Through the window of my railway compartment I see beautiful buildings on the skyline of the low hills to the south. I turn to the old man who is sitting quietly in the corner and, miming, ask him what they are. "San Luca," he replies. I quickly write the name down and refer to my guide book. It tells me that the Basilica de San Luca is one of the great sights of Bologna, reached via a row of 666 arcaded porticos, and gives a magnificent view of the city and the Appenines. I wonder whether I ought to interrupt my journey and visit Bologna. It certainly gets a good write up in the book. The trouble is that cities are busy, noisy and dirty, which is why I fled from Milan after only three hours yesterday. I decide that Bologna can wait, and as the train pulls into the station I sit tight. The man leaves, shutting the compartment door behind him. I am alone.

She enters the compartment almost before I realise the door has been opened. Dark skinned, she looks like Romany with her patterned, full-length simple skirt and creamy coloured blouse decorated with rose buds. Her hair is black, but with highlights which suggest henna. She takes a headscarf from her blue plastic carrier bag and wraps it expertly around her hair, pulling it away from the nape of her neck and forehead. She slips off her worn sandals, swings her feet up and lies across the three seats opposite me. She is on her right side, her left arm in a v across her chest, the hand cushioning her head on the carrier bag. Her right arm is flung outwards, wrist uppermost. Within a few seconds she has taken over the compartment. People walk down the corridor, pause, look in, and move on. She has made the compartment ours.

The train moves out. The views from the window begin again once we leave the confines of the city, but I find myself inexorably drawn to studying her. I become aware of her smell, faint but palpable, sharp even, in the warm compartment. It is not from a bottle. Nothing bought from a perfumery would smell like this. It is not unpleasant, but vaguely sensual. It is a womanly smell mingled with a trace of tobacco and something elusive. I struggle for a while to find a word that identifies it, and eventually find nothing works except 'earthy'. No, not 'earthy' but 'of the earth', a musty, lemony smell that causes me to move the saliva in my mouth as though she has brought with her the aroma of a lifetime's work on the land, of digging, planting, watering, harvesting, of growing up, of having children. I tell myself I am romanticising, but, with the aroma, the feeling persists.

Her feet are brown, sunburned, with lighter strips indicating the constant wearing of the same sandals as she has just abandoned. Toenails are dirty, and smudges of dirt and dust are visible between her toes. The dirt seems natural however and it does not offend or repulse me. Around her left ankle she wears an elasticated string of pale red beads. Under her skirt I glimpse the plain blue of a petticoat. Her out-flung arm is pale from the inner wrist to the elbow crease, but the fingers are half curled around a dirty palm. One finger, the third, is roughly bandaged with a piece of blue cloth that may have come from her petticoat. She breathes regularly and deeply, and I feel she could probably sleep anywhere. In repose she looks very young, with a wide nose and full, generous lips.

I doze and the train slips through the Appenines, high wooded hills and green valleys, and then we spill out onto a plain with a blanket of red roofed houses and apartment blocks, a river alongside, looking lifeless and torpid, beaten into submission by the heat. Prato Stazione, a clean station with no sign of life on either platform. Then the train slows and we enter Firenze. Still she sleeps.

Firenze is busy, as is to be expected at the height of the tourist season. The corridor is alive with travellers and luggage, but no-one enters. They look at me, at the sleeping form of my companion stretched over the seats, and move on. It remains our compartment. A few moments after the train leaves the station, with an excellent sense of timing, she opens her eyes, stretches without a trace of self consciousness and sits up. Ignoring me, she fumbles in the folds of her skirt, produces a cigarette, and vanishes into the corridor for a smoke.

On returning, she starts to fiddle with the blue

rag on her finger. I notice that dried blood has stained both sides of her hand. I point to the rag and shrug interrogatively. She mimes cutting and holds the finger high, pinching it at the base to indicate bleeding. I rummage in my rucksack producing a large first aid plaster and some wet wipes and offer them, half expecting them to be turned down but she doesn't. instead she takes them immediately, saying "Gracie." As the rag comes off, the cut appears. It is ugly and deep and swollen, the edges arced wide apart, almost exposing the bone. The pain of it is so obvious that I can almost feel it pulsing. She is utterly intent on it, cleaning it first and then using the plaster to try and draw it together. She winces with a sharp intake of breath several times. When she is finished she throws the rag and wet wipes out the window and lies down again.

The trolley waiter throws open the compartment door. He is young, handsome and by the look of his forearms and wide shoulders, a body builder, a weight trainer. He wants to be a man's man, do a man's job. Trolley waiting on a train is not for him. He treats neither of us as customers, disdainfully overriding my attempts to sort my lira out, taking the appropriate notes from my hand without being invited to do so. She buys a can of Heineken and he turns to go. She says something, but he ignores her. She repeats it, sharper this time, no nonsense in her tone, and his matriarchal inheritance overcomes him. He reaches reluctantly onto the trolley and gives her a plastic glass. "Gracie," she says, and dismissively closes the door on him. She rummages in her bag and produces some foil that is wrapped around a white bread sandwich. She offers me a bite. I decline with a smile. She eats and drinks, then retires to the corridor for another cigarette. I find myself wishing I smoked.

When she returns she points at me and says "Roma?" I nod and repeat the question at her. She nods but then indicates that she will change trains there. I ask, "Roma then ....?"

"Campoleone," she replies. I start to look through my dictionary, but she leans forward and, using the guide book, indicates that Campoleone is just south of Rome. "Figlia, nipote. In Campoleone." Daughter, grandson, my dictionary translates for me.

Rome, about two hours before dusk. The train swings clockwise around the city to the main terminal and she vanishes whilst I am retrieving my rucksack from above the seat. The station is thronged, individuals, families, tourists, residents, guards, polizei, caribinieri, and constant sound. I spend some time trying to identify the train I wish to catch tomorrow, but cannot concentrate for the noise and bustle. I leave and cross to the grassy area outside the museum. I study my guide book, wondering where to unroll my sleeping bag in the eternal city. After several minutes I become aware of a whistle blowing. I turn, and a woman in uniform removes the whistle from her mouth and makes it plain that sitting on the grass is 'vietare'. I move on.

I walk a few blocks, turn left and at the end of the road there is the Colosseum. It seems immense, and as I walk towards it I am already wondering if I could somehow sleep close by and get the feel of it early in the morning. But the crowds are milling about, groups of students, of scouts, guides, religious groups, adults, all being lectured on Roman history and everywhere rubbish, discarded cartons, papers, drinks cans. Feral cats prowl through the bushes and grass, scavenging. It's appalling. I become more and more depressed, and my rucksack grows heavier. It is now dark. I contemplate using a hotel, but the prices are exorbitant.

My only food has been a mid morning sandwich, and I decide to eat. I find a Sicilian restaurant 'The Trattoria' on Via Magnanapoli.   I feel my energy return with my first sip of red wine and have a good meal, which restores ordered thinking.   I do not want to stay in Rome. It is awful. So where? The country, the earth? The woman. A name flashes into my brain. Campoleone. I pay for my food, shrug on my rucksack and stride out for the station.

It is 15 minutes short of midnight. I check a timetable. There is a train leaving in five minutes. Unbelievable. I use the automatic ticket dispenser to buy my ticket, and race onto the platform. The train is still there. I check with a guard and he nods. I settle in my compartment, and feel content.

Four youngsters tumble into the compartment, two boys, two girls. I suddenly realise they are talking english. It's days since I talked with anyone in english. My first instinct is to ignore them, but the desire to converse is great. A few minutes after the train pulls out from the station, I move across to speak. They are from Manchester, travelling through Europe on Inter Rail passes for a month. I feel slightly jealous of the opportunities these young people have nowadays. They have a certain amount of courage, for they are heading out of the city with no clear idea of where they will sleep.

Their initial suspicion of me fades, and they tell me they slept on the station the previous night because Rome did not feel safe. Courageous, and sensible as well. I am aware that one of the girls is subjecting me to quizzical glances. I am certain she is wondering what an old man like me is doing travelling around like this, on his own. I am almost certainly older than her father, and definitely look it at present. I hear one of the others address her as Emma.

I return to my seat and leave them to their conversations and music. After a few minutes the lights go out. I look out at the night and feel the cool of the dark air and know it is good to be out of the city. I lean out of the window occasionally and watch for my station. After half an hour I see it approaching. The lights are still out so, as I shoulder my rucksack, I say 'goodbye' into the darkness, and they reply in kind. Then through the dark, just before I step out of the compartment, Emma's voice adds, "Good travelling." There is a slight wistfulness in the tone that betrays she is on the cusp of understanding - to savour the uncertainty of the experience, to follow the whim, to travel alone.

Five people, me included, get off at Campoleone. I have to climb down onto the track as my carriage does not quite make the platform. It is a long walk to the exit. The village beyond the station is utterly still and dark. I have made a good choice. I think of the woman on the train. I do not know where I am heading but I walk briskly from the station in case any caribinieri are sitting in a car watching.

After a few minutes I turn up a road alongside the primary school. At the top of a short hill it turns left. On that side, a row of dark, detached, shuttered houses continue into the velvet folds of the distance. On the right I can make out fields. I walk and, as I pass, dogs bark. I wait until I pass a house where no dog barks, and then turn right. I am immediately in a vineyard. The foliage overhead lays a broken pattern of moonlight on the soft ground. I move a short distance and lie down, just as I am, head on my rucksack, on the earth.

A mosquito homes in on my body heat. When its whine stops, I slap. A dog barks. So the house does have a dog. It might have missed me first time but it knows I am here now. It announces this to everyone and I tense up. Over several minutes, as I lie immobile, it gradually quietens. I am glad it is behind the fence and wall of the house. I doze off, then roll over. The dog barks. I curse quietly. I resolve to move when the animal is distracted elsewhere. When the opportunity arises I pace deeper into the vineyard. This time I lay my bivouac bag down properly and wriggle into my sleeping bag.

Through the vines I recognise Gemini. A half moon is good for recognising constellations, for its light is sufficient to blot out the lesser stars whilst accentuating those of greater magnitude. Then I feel sleep rolling over me, a soporific ground swell of ebbing consciousness and I am gone, down into the soft smelling earth.

I sleep soundly for a few hours then awake, just after dawn, and swiftly pack. I walk through the vines eating a handful of half full grapes to sharpen my mouth after sleep. As I emerge onto the dusty white road, there is the dog, black with pointed ears, young. It is not in the garden, but outside. The beat it patrols is obvious in the flattened grass and compacted soil around the perimeter wall and fence. It barks furiously but does not move. I suddenly comprehend. It is like us. It is afraid of things it does not know or understand; afraid of the dark, of shadows in the vineyard. I ignore it. It does not follow me.

The station is deserted, but I translate the hand

written sign at the ticket office with my dictionary, and follow the instructions to a cafe a short distance away. It is open, just, and my ticket to Pozzuoli costs twice as much as my first espresso of this August Sunday.

I have over two hours to wait. On the platform I lie on a convex blue bench and write, as the sun comes up and Campoleone comes to life. It is a good place, where people laugh in early morning conversations, where the station master waters the plants between trains arriving and departing; where the early morning grapes taste sharp and clean, where dogs are scared of the dark and the dark is patterned by the night sky.

The sun warms my back and shoulders as I write swiftly, my thoughts tumbling from the pen. As I finish, I look up, along the rails into the past and future, to where they merge into one. It all feels good, complete, whole. There is a symmetry to it beyond understanding and my eyes fill with tears at the losing of it. The tears are sharp on my senses, their salt sharp on my lips. I realise that my tears are like the grapes, and like the people - of the earth.

My train appears, approaches. I do not want to arrive.

Goff takes Giles canoeing on a historic river.

Eureka!" echoed over the waters of the Oklawaha River as the frontiersmen strained on their paddles and steered onto the sandy beach.

Haunted by insects, wary of reptiles, at the limits of their endurance, they had urged their way upstream, tantalised by a horizon never further than the next river bend, forced onwards by impenetrable riverbank foliage, this sudden clearing was their oasis. Their cry of relief and triumph lived on as the name of a settlement which became a thriving mid 19th to early 20th century ferry terminal on this, the first highway in and out of central Florida.

Eureka is history now, a listless, sun hammered scattering of buildings. Interstate 75 lies just to the west, the new highway conveying citrus and farm produce from the Sunshine State to Georgia and

29

beyond. But to understand a little of what those frontiersmen had endured, Eureka is the place to access the river.

Skeins of mist, as yet unraveled by the morning sun were draped along the dense riverbanks as we curled our toes through liquid sand and launched our canoe into the current. Somewhat apprehensive, our ill-defined forebodings reached out and linked us for the first time to those pioneers. However, with movement came a confidence developed by the rhythm of our strokes, and the bow cleaved the biscuit coloured waters as we powered upstream. When the sun found our shoulders we left the last of our fears in the slow eddies of this Seminole Indian river.

Lake Griffin is some 50 miles north west of Orlando, and from it emerges the Oklawaha, flowing northwards to eventually join the St Johns River, south of Jacksonville. For much of its length its eastern banks form the boundary of the Ocala National Forest.

This forest, thick with oak, pine, cedar and cypress surrounded us as we travelled towards Silver Springs, a five hour journey. During that time we passed no significant landing place, nor people. We saw young terrapins warming themselves on driftwood and watched them scatter like handfuls of thrown gravel as we approached, and we paddled away from tiny alligators taking the sun, just in case larger ones were keeping a red eye on them and us.

A score of miles later, a road bridge confirmed

our arrival at Silver Springs, where the world's largest artesian well system pours a billion gallons daily into the Oklawaha. For us a small tributary beckoned, whose current inexorably bore us back into our apprehensions as we forced our way through entangling growth and forest debris. Insects hummed a constant appreciation of our exposed limbs; a Cottonmouth snake introduced itself by opening its jaws at us. Our first intimation of the large alligator was when it rolled from its rotting tree trunk into the water, a canoe's length away. Giles back-paddled furiously as he was in the bow of the canoe.

Hours later, tired, bitten and hungry, we rejoined the main river and drifted downstream beneath a King's ransom of stars. In the velvet darkness a clearing materialised. The canoe grounded on sand. Now we understood. Eureka!

I wrote this about 15 years ago although the actual event took place in 1993. I was fortunate enough to enjoy a period of working in Florida delivering management training programmes for Florida Power and Light Company, the major Utilities Company. The venue was a couple of hours drive north of Orlando, a rustic and remote area of sandy 'roads' not far from the river mentioned in the story. Never one to waste an opportunity, I borrowed a canoe, intending to explore the river on my day off, and was then asked by a young man who was working with me if he could accompany me. Giles had never canoed before, and so he had to come in my vessel, and I took the stern, whilst he knelt up front. As we negotiated the tributary we spotted the alligator dozing on the fallen tree. I was eager to get as close as possible, but Giles, not unnaturally, for he was in the bow, was less than enthusiastic. I seem to recall that as I paddled forwards he was paddling backwards!

Home Waters - Getting to Know Joe

My son Joe and I sat in the softness of the Hebridean night, just the two of us, drinking our hot chocolate. On a cruise that had proved to be a constant source of enjoyment and challenge, this day had been the culmination of all the events leading up to it. Now, wrapped in the quiet euphoria of achievement and experiences, I was content and had no wish to be anywhere else in the world.....

It had all started in London in 1995. The City. Hard pavements, anonymous faces. Mobile phone-

again. But this time a family call. "Dad?" As though he couldn't quite believe his luck. "It's me, Joe." My youngest, 20 years old, a canoeing instructor in France – or so I thought.

"Joe?" My voice must have reflected my surprise in hearing his voice, for he quickly took charge of the conversation. "Dad, I'm in a phone box and I haven't got much money. What time are you leaving London?" My reply pleased him and he responded

33

swiftly. "I'm at Euston station now. Look out for me at the ticket office" and his voice vanished.

Our rail journey north provided him with the opportunity to treat me to a resumé of his brief career in the activity holiday industry, a story that cost me his rail fare home, as he was, of course, penniless.

He looked good, very bronzed and fit, and I enjoyed being associated with him, despite the disparity of appearances. My suit and briefcase looked stuffy against his jeans, tee shirt and rucksack. We did match hair styles though, as he'd shaved his hair off, whilst mine had vanished unaided a long time previously. When I asked what he intended to do for the rest of the summer he shrugged and, irritating as always, responded with his own question, "What are you doing?"

"Three weeks solo on the boat," I replied. "I'm going up on Saturday."

He thought for a moment and then surprised me. "Can I come with you?" Joe was a natural in the outdoors, but as a youngster he had never been enthusiastic for even the shortest of sailing trips. So I was cautious in my reply, repeating that it was a long time away and that I intended, weather permitting, to go north towards Skye. He eventually convinced me that he really wanted to come, and, decision made, it felt good to contemplate spending time with him.

'Pegasus' is moored at the head of Loch Goil north of the Clyde and we arrived in early evening sunshine. After ferrying stores and gear we remained on the mooring that night. Next morning, fair winds and sunshine coaxed our 8 metre yacht as far as the small anchorage of Callum's Hole, Bute, where no swell disturbed our sleep.

Enjoying a mug of tea whilst listening to the first Inshore Waters forecast of the day I experienced the calming effect that living aboard always induces in me, for, with the exception of weather and tides, all other concerns gradually fall astern and vanish. I allowed the radio to progress from maritime forecasts to Farming Today as the pearl mist of the morning lightened with the promised settled weather. Joe slept on and I resisted the temptation to waken him as the sports bulletin reported a news item about his favourite football team.

An hour later sunshine burst through the last of the mist and beamed into the cabin. Joe stirred and stretched and when he sat up I gave him a mug of tea. We chatted and made leisurely plans with the radio still providing a background of news. When sport featured again it repeated the item about Liverpool FC and he suddenly sat bolt upright and said "That's amazing. I dreamed that. That really is incredible." He looked disappointed as I suggested that he must have heard it subconsciously 90 minutes earlier, and the incident provided a touchstone for a smile and a joke throughout the day as we crossed towards Arran where we picked up a mooring in Brodick Bay.

Joe sunbathed, then went ashore whilst I pottered with simple chores aboard, and when the day cooled we donned running shoes and shorts to ascend Goat Fell. He ran alongside me patiently until the final few hundred metres, then eased effortlessly away. From the summit we watched the sun slide towards the Kintyre peninsular before commencing a long, fluid descent of Glen Rosa, and we bathed in the burn before returning to Pegasus.

Sanda Island next, another fine day and good sailing, followed by a run around the island. We agreed to round the Mull of Kintyre on the early morning tide and I made porridge before we turned in, ready for the prompt start.

In the pre light we lifted anchor and motored in windless conditions with the log trailed. It became obvious that our eagerness to be under way, combined with the favourable tide was going to deliver us to the Mull early. The 10 miles swept under the keel in little over an hour, twice the speed recorded on the log, and sunrise clearly illuminated what appeared to be miniature haystacks and steeples on the horizon. Joe, a little cold and bored, vanished below and heated the porridge, and when I declined my share he sat at the cabin table to do justice to his breakfast. Barely had he lifted the first spoonful when we entered the overfalls. The spoon missed its destination, the bowl took off and landed in his lap and he gave out a howl of anger and surprise, followed by immediate recriminations. "You did that on purpose," he yelled up at me. I protested my innocence and suggested he take a look around, and offered him the tiller if he felt he could do better. He viewed the size and randomness of the steepling waves for a few seconds and decided he would leave it to me. Within fifteen minutes we were through, more porridge was made, and as we turned north a good breeze set in as the sun warmed our shoulders.

As the days passed I learned how to work effectively with my son. I involved him in the decision making and offered up options and ideas rather than commands. On the foredeck he made the decisions that involved him and told me what he required from me to enable him to carry out his role efficiently. We slipped into a relationship that was companionable and comfortable, and I rediscovered a filial love that had been submerged for much of his teenage period and all the time the sun shone, anchorages proved safe and fresh breezes moved us north. We sailed, we ran, we fished and ate what we caught. Islay, Colonsay, Luing came and went. Pegasus had the white bit between her teeth as we galloped up the Sound of Mull and overnighted at Tobermory. After Ardnamurchan Point a whole new cruising ground opened up. And still the sun shone.

From a secure anchorage in Loch Scresort we tore our fingers to pieces on the rough gabbro of Rum's rocky ridges and bathed in a burn so cold that we stopped breathing for a lifetime of seconds.

Tantalisingly close were Skye's black ridges of the Cuillin, but with two of our three weeks gone, regretfully it was time to turn for home.

As if to mirror our mood, the next morning was leaden, with a fretful breeze and lumpy sea. We lurched across towards Arisaig, wallowing at times until, close to the entrance to the Sound we started the engine. To starboard the 50' launch 'Shearwater' was also approaching, returning from its ferry run to Eigg. Joe watched it for several seconds, then sniffed. "His exhaust fumes smell strong." I agreed, and noted how persistent the smell was as Shearwater drew ahead of us. Realisation dawned. "It's not his boat smelling, it's ours!'

I looked over the stern and my suspicions were confirmed by the lack of water emerging from our own exhaust. We edged into a rocky gap on the lee of the peninsular, dropped anchor in 2 metres where I stripped down the cooling system, blew it through with the dinghy pump, reassembled it, whereupon, despite finding nothing amiss, it worked perfectly.

A little over an hour had elapsed but in that time the breeze had hardened into a brisk southerly. We agreed that we could sail up the couple of miles of twisting but well marked channel and as the broad bay opened up we made out a great number of yachts moored off the village. Joe requested the engine, and bagged the foresail as we eased our way between several boats. The wind was touching 20 knots now and with the anchor down we left the engine ticking over for several minutes before turning it off.

Joe announced his intention of going ashore, and he joked that he wouldn't need to row as he cast off the stern. I went below and lifted the cabin sole to sponge out water that had drained from the engine whilst I had been clearing the cooling system. Suddenly Pegasus reared and plunged backwards, dragging chain and anchor. A frenzy of activity followed all in the space of seconds that seemed like hours. Even with the engine engaged Pegasus was almost impossible to manage, and relief flooded over me as Joe suddenly appeared at my side, ran to the bow and heaved armfuls of chain up. Pegasus quieted immediately, and we found a vacant mooring where we sorted ourselves out. I gave him a rueful smile. "I wouldn't have coped without you. I was starting to panic."

He grinned. "I saw her start to drag." His grin became a laugh. "I nearly left you to it. I didn't fancy rowing back in that wind, and I thought you'd cope. But you didn't appear to be." He laughed again. "I shipped a lot of water in the dinghy, and got pretty wet."

The following morning we headed south and stopped briefly at Iona. Then, in soft winds that failed to shift an enveloping sea mist, we breasted the long, soporific swells between Mull and Colonsay. Pegasus rippled along at no more than a couple of knots. With no horizons our environment induced a sense of detachment in which we seemed suspended, timeless. Joe fell asleep in the cabin as the afternoon eased by and I eventually gave him a nudge before the evening shipping forecast. Waiting for him to take the tiller, I noticed a white plastic bag floating just below the surface off the starboard quarter and wondered whether it had been something similar that had fouled our engine intake. Suddenly the bag appeared to accelerate and overtake us. Briefly disoriented by this optical illusion I was still trying to make sense of it when the 'bag' metamorphosed into a large Minke whale which broke surface alongside. My shout of concern and excitement rocketed Joe into the cockpit. Initially nervous, we realised there was nothing we could do apart from enjoy a rare opportunity to watch this wonderful mammal as it crossed and re-crossed from one side of Pegasus to the other. We estimated it to be about two thirds of the length of the boat, and it stayed with us for several minutes.

Its eventual departure left us keenly disappointed, but the images of its visit were engraved in our memories, and we found our awareness and perceptions of our environment immeasurably heightened by the experience. We would look at each other and start smiling and then start talking about it all over again. Everything around us that evening seemed so much sharper, and we marvelled at the contrast between the grey rain squalls that raced over Colonsay whilst further east the quartzite Paps of Jura stood gleaming in the sun.

Not wanting the day to end we took the flood tide through Islay Sound, making 10 knots in the darkness, the steady pulse of the engine reassuring beneath our bare feet. On the eastern tip of Islay is the small anchorage of Aros Bay, and we worked our way towards it through a combination of speed over ground, use of the depth gauge, and the two lighthouses, Ardmore light off the bow and McArthur's light astern. Long after midnight we felt our way into the anchorage. Reluctant to lose the glow of such a momentous day we lingered in the cockpit with our mugs of chocolate, reliving it all again.

After three hours sleep I sneaked up on deck and was delighted to see we had anchored in the exact centre of the small bay. Joe joined me and we decided that we'd make the most of the wind and sunshine to head around the Mull. The conditions remained ideal and an 18 hour sail ended as we crept into Lamlash Bay, again anchoring in the dark. The following morning the outside world began to intrude into our existence, phone calls to family reminding us of other priorities and responsibilities. We coasted northwards to Dunoon, where my elder son joined us for an evening meal, before leaving Joe and I for our final night aboard.

Joe had one more mountain run, from Ardentinny over and along the several miles of the

Carrick ridge to our home mooring. Even here the sun still shone as we worked efficiently alongside each other, cleaning Pegasus down. We ferried our gear ashore, and finally looked back at her, lying easy to her mooring. "Nice one, Joe?" Half statement, half question, reluctant to let go. He took his time, three weeks of memories behind his gaze across the water towards Pegasus, and then "Yeah. A good one, dad," and he confirmed it with a smile that matched the sun. "Thanks."

Aberfan

The horror of it awoke that childhood nightmare of drowning, a black emotional gasping panic of fear. Tearless in suffocating water for you can't cry underwater. The memory was equalled only by the event itself. It was a day of relentless rain and heavy grey cloud that advanced from the west, and the weather interrupted my military training at the R.A.F. School of parachuting near Oxford. so the early finish provided an opportunity to head for home and a weekend with family and friends.

Even as it got dark I was standing in the damp of an October evening in my uniform, on the side of the A40 trunk road with my thumb pointing towards Wales. A lorry stopped in a shower of spray. I clambered into the cab, not caring to enquire where it was heading. The driver soon dampened my relief at being warm and out of the rain, for Newport was as close to Barry as he could get me. I made no comment, and we were soon underway going in the right direction. The obligation was on me, the hitchhiker, to make the conversation, but before I could say anything he brought me up to speed with the tragic news of the day. I was staring down the two yellow tunnels of the headlights watching the rain bounce off the tarmac as he told me of a tragedy in the Welsh valleys, where a coal tip had avalanched and engulfed a primary school. A place called Aberfan, and as I heard the name my memory unrolled a list of village names.

As a teenager, myself and a group of friends would drive up into the Brecon Beacons every Sunday. We went the same way each weekend, driving north across the Welsh coalfield, passing through mining village after village with the Pit Wheels usually stationary above the greedy shafts that dropped vertically to the black gold of the Welsh coal syncline that stretched from Merthyr to Taff s Wells. None of the sleeping miners in those hamlets that we drove through would have felt sympathy or envy for the one activity that engaged us in the limestone strata north of Dowlais Top, for we enjoyed caving, exploring the water-carved passages of the cave systems. On sunny days we sometimes climbed on the limestone quarries whose rock had fed the smelting furness of the Dowlais

Iron works. But we often just stretched our legs and expanded our lungs on the green slopes of the Brecon Beacons.

The names of the village became as familiar as the names on the class register in School days. Once beyond Taff's Wells the villages all appeared to be stapled to the ground by the gantries of the Pit Wheels. Treforest, GlynTaff, Cilfynydd, and onwards, ignoring the turning for Pontypridd and still northwards, taking the Merthyr road not the Aberdare turning. The sweeping bend in the road through Quakers Yard, then Treharriss that always made me think of the Harris brothers who were in school with me. Through Pen-y-Graig and Mt.Pleasant, then Troed y Rhiw, these names became a Poem of Welsh words, a litany of settlements tracing the industrial development and exploitation of the valley.

In the dark cab of that lorry, going to Newport, the mists and fog of time dissipated and I recalled the name on the road sign pointing down a small turning to the left shortly after Mt. Pleasant. It became clear in my mind – Aberfan. Suddenly I knew where this tragedy had happened. My friends and I had driven above the village frequently, on our way to the hills, to breath. On the hill above Aberfan a fresh water spring had lubricated the slag from the local mine so that it too could breathe again.

So here in the Merthyr valley, the valley of the Martyr below the town of Merthyr Tydfil, named after a princess slain by pagans almost 1,500 years ago. The pagan followers of mammon extracted a price from the local populace far greater than a single princess, for the black gold that was Welsh coal. One hundred and forty four people were martyred, one hundred and fourteen of them children. Ancient fairy tales often told of evil dragons who demanded that villages should surrender their children as a price for being left in peace by the voracious dragon.

It was half way through the Christmas term and thus for many of the youngest children these were their first ever school days. If the children ever looked up from the school playground in those early days of learning, their horizon was dominated by the slag heap with its own railway for the mine's trams carrying load after load of slag that was dumped ever higher. Half way up the hillside the spring breathed in and out that black Friday in October. It was a month before Armistice day.

A depression formed in the tip as the spring breathed in. And then it breathed out, black and pagan it rose up out of its own pit and turned itself into a wall of water, a tsunami of material hewn from the bowels of the valley of the Martyr.

Now almost exactly 48 years later I visit the cemetery on the slope of Mynydd Merthyr above the village. The rows of symmetrical white headstones resemble a First World War cemetery. My friend and I move slowly along the rows. It is difficult to talk.

Emotion generated an internal spring of salty tears as we read the headstones that mark the resting places of son, daughter, brother and brother, sister and brother all so terribly young.

In this year that marks the centenary of the start of the war to end all wars it is a Poet from that conflict who has written the words that expressed my feelings on that hill side of the Martyrs.

'My heart was shaken with tears and horror' wrote Siegfried Sassoon. My imagination provoked tears as I experienced the horror of their deaths. These poor souls had no chance, in Dylan Thomas' words, to 'Rage, rage against the dying of the light' as the school was engulfed by that black wave.

Some Bird

Her demeanour, her whole stance was one of confidence. No, it was more than that. She exuded a predatory arrogance. Not even the fact that she was the intruder, the trespasser caught in the act of preparing her breakfast on the barbeque stove in the open garage caused her the slightest embarrassment. She stood so still that for a moment she seemed to be a mannequin and for several seconds we could not believe our eyes. But that frozen hesitation on her part was her only concession to being compromised by what she obviously viewed as our intrusion into her space.

Oh yes, she was proud all right, scared of no one. When she turned her head it was a regal movement, nothing furtive or guilty about the disdainful look with which she regarded us. Her baleful eyes, iris yellow and black at their core challenged us as to whose rights were being infringed. There was no fear in that gaze. The beautiful breast, dark horizontal bars across soft white plumage led our gaze downwards to her yellow legs and thus to the evidence. For scattered around her splayed, dark talons were the feathers and down of a small songbird, the remains of which were bleeding onto the stove.

Long, still moments passed. Impasse. Us, reluctant to forego this tableau of still life and death; she, unwilling to concede sovereignty of her chosen plucking and eating post. Until, finally, her impatience and hunger caused her to launch herself down, sweeping low and soundlessly past us, the carcass held high in one talon, out into the indifferent sunlight of the pecking order of the silent day.

A Leap of Faith

I remember that it was the Saturday evening before Easter Sunday. I had been home for just a few days, on leave from 43 Commando Royal Marines. I was sitting in the Living room with my father, the first time I had seen him since Christmas time. He was a very committed Christian who had wanted to train as a minister when he was younger. His faith had impacted on family life when I was a small boy. The family went to church every week and Sunday school was a must. When I became a teenager I was not allowed out on a Sunday evening unless I attended Evensong first. None of these constraints on my personal time endeared me to religion. At the age of 19 I announced my intention to join the Royal Marines. My father did not take well to his son being trained to kill people. After I left home and commenced the rigorous training he eventually showed a lot of interest in what I was experiencing and the skills I was learning. My increasing maturity and his interest brought about a great improvement in our relationship. Whilst home on leaves I sometimes attended an occasional church service with him, and this pleased him.

As we sat together on that Easter Saturday I was telling him about the mountaineering in North Wales, and the cliff climbing in Cornwall. He then asked what the immediate future held for me. I slid down on to the carpet, in front of the fire that he had lit take the chill off the room. "I have to report to a small aerodrome on Salisbury Plain, a place called Netheravon to be trained as a Freefall parachutist." He paused for a moment and then said, "I thought you had already trained as a parachutist?" So I explained that as a free fall jumper I would be expected to leave the plane or helicopter at a greater height, and fall until I was about 2,000ft above the ground, and then open my parachute myself rather than relying on a rip-cord attached to the aircraft. And I told him the Instructor joke. 'Pull your ripcord when the cows look about the size of a dog. But if the dogs are the same size as a cow, you have left it to late.' "Rather you than me," he said. And I smiled at his next question, thinking it was prompted at the thought of just falling out of an aeroplane. "Do you still go to church?" I replied with the truth, that I didn't, but I knew this would disappoint him. So I added that I still considered myself a Christian. "But are you?"

He came forward and knelt alongside me. He reached for the fire tongs and lifted a cherry red piece of coal off the fire and laid it in the hearth. "Watch it." He said to me. As the coal cooled it lost its colour and heat. My father spoke again. "And that's what happens to us if we move away from the fireplace of our faith. But faith can be rekindled by all manner of things." He continued, "I read an article recently that quoted some examples. One man confessed that on hearing a particular piece of classical music he had realised that the composer's talent must surely be a God given talent. A new parent had related how the beautiful structure of his child's ear had inspired him to acknowledge the exaction of a God."

The following morning I attended the Easter service with my father. I could sense his pride and joy at having me alongside him. I enjoyed that feeling more than I enjoyed the service, although some of the Welsh hymn tunes reached into me to nurture the parts of me that the service did not touch. We emerged into a wet and cold day. Later that day I packed my stuff so that I could leave promptly the next morning for Salisbury Plain. What a blank and feature less place the plain is, ideal for an aerodrome.

For the next couple of days the ground training went well and the prospect of the first jump filled my horizon. I was awoken a couple of mornings later by the instructor. "Jump day Bird Man! The weather is good, so get yourself organised and be in the hanger ready to go at 0600. I looked at my watch, it was 0500. I felt nervous and excited. An hour later the pilot, the instructor and myself walked across the dew-covered grass to the aircraft. The pilot climbed in first, followed by the instructor, whose job was to act as spotter and dispatcher. I was the last one to climb in. As my feet left terra firma I looked back and saw the three sets of footprints clear in the dewy grass. The dispatch sat close to the gap where the door should have been with his back to the pilot. I sat on the floor opposite the dispatch.

The pilot fired up the engines and the cabin was filled with noise and the smell of high-octane fuel. We taxied across to the head of the grass runway. The pilot gunned the engines and released the brakes. As we accelerated down the green strip the wheels threw up a dewy curtain of moisture. Then the tyres left the ground, and we climbed into the morning sky, and the wing I could see glinted and shone silver in the rays of the rising sun, as it seeped and elbowed itself over the eastern horizon.

The propeller that I could see chopped these rays into a kaleidoscope of spinning rainbow blocks. Far below the greening spring country unrolled. Fingers of mist highlighted the lines of streams and a river. The mist spilled out of the hollows and depressions of the land below us. Tentacles of mist reached out along the hedgerows and over low-lying ground. In the hedges and in the branches of the few trees the grey mist hung like skeins of wool. We passed over a small circle of what appeared to be tree stumps, dark against the grey of the mist that had woven itself around them.

Even as we passed 6,000 ft. over the top of them the first of the rising sun's spears of gold lanced through the monument. woodhenge, site of ancient worship, brought to life by the power and promise of the sun in the East. In a few seconds its spiritual impact was lost as we continued our south-westerly course. Below us the black top surface of a major trunk road led my eyes directly to the massive structure of Stonehenge. Again the light from the east brought the huge mass of the structure to life. It was a pagan pageant of shadows and light. The joy of life and the beauty of our world flooded through me. The plane banked as the pilot gained more height and turned to take a line that would bring us over the drop zone. Again my view changed and, once again, I glimpsed another monument to the glory of the east. A few miles to the south-east a bank of mist was shot through with the gold of the dawning day. Piercing this was the steeple of Salisbury Cathedral. The shadow of the steeple stretched out away from the east on its 'eiderdown' of mist. As the warmth of the sun melted the mist the steeple assumed it full stature.

The plane was now approaching the drop zone and the dispatcher signalled me to get ready. My mouth was dry as I slid forward. I stepped out onto the wing as I grasped the wings strut. The dispatcher tapped me on the shoulder and I launched myself backwards. The world spins about me. I glimpse Stonehenge again briefly as I fell. I felt no fear, but a feeling of belonging was palpable. I belonged here, cushioned in this air that was imbued with historical faiths and beliefs. I watch my altimeter unwind as I fell. Then at 2,500 feet I arched my body and reached for my ripcord handle. I felt the chute peel off my back, and, as the canopy developed, I felt the snatch of the harness at my shoulders. I floated down and steered myself to land near the hanger. I could see the footprints in the dewy grass left by the three of us less than an hour before but, as I counted them, there now appeared to be four sets of prints. I find myself wondering, was it my father walking with me when I was in the cathedral of the dawn sky? Footprints, freefall and faith. That evening I wrote to my father and told him of my leap of faith.

DAD

Timbuktu was looking for a town to twin with in 2002! There is but one place that fits the bill and that is Barry Docks in South Wales and that is my mother's doing. Her romantic nature had woven magic around Timbuktu that was much stronger than her sense of geography. She loved the sea and the idea of travelling, and so my early years were spent walking around the docks and lock gates of my hometown in her company. As the cargo ships loaded with Welsh coal eased out into the Bristol Channel, my query as to "Where's that one going, Mum?' always elicited the same wistful response, "Timbuktu and over the horizon." If she knew this mystical African city was not only 1,400 kms from the nearest sea but also on the edge of the Sahara and thus probably not needing coal, Welsh or otherwise, she didn't share that knowledge with me.

No astrology column ever escaped her attention; she trawled through them daily and frequently managed to make the facts fit the forecasts. Her purse always held a four-leafed clover for luck, and she never turned a 'clothes peg-peddling' gypsy away from the door. The reward for buying from the gypsy was always a flattering fortune telling, and she confided in me after one reading that one of her grand children was destined to be a doctor. When my first-born arrived, born on her birthday and was christened David Rhys, thus D.R. Todd, as far as my mother was concerned that was another prediction come true. Her ability to weave her way into the lives of her two grandsons was manifested by dying on the day David's brother was born.

Her romantic nature was at odds with the pragmatic christianity of my father, and during the late 1950's the marriage began to show the strains of two people going in different directions. She began to sleep downstairs, ostensibly because it eased her asthmatic problems, but in reality because she preferred it. She rather sarcastically christened him 'The Major' after a character in a TV Western series. He missed the sarcasm and enjoyed his elevated status. Perhaps most damaging of all she labeled him a hypochondriac, a tag that was more than a little unfair as he was a self employed baker who worked hard and long, going without holidays for years on end. He would be lighting the back furnace at 5 am, and covering the dough troughs filled with the next day's mix well after 10p.m after selling the bread from his small van during the day. His one bad experience of pleurisy and a hospitalization with ulcers hardly warranted being called a hypochondriac but as a youngster it was impossible for me to be objective, living with what had become a dysfunctional relationship, and so sides were taken.

Mum said he was a hypochondriac, therefore he must be, and as dad approached 60 and was diagnosed with angina this seemed to confirm everything she had suspected of him. He took to having what he termed '40 winks' after lunch, lying on the couch in the lounge, spectacles placed carefully on the coffee table alongside. When I chose to follow a career in the Royal Marines she backed me to the hilt, revelling in the idea of vicariously seeing the world, whilst Dad grappled with the moral issue of bearing arms. Mum enjoyed my travels, and my letters home prompted her to write her own replies several times a month. These letters were all about the weather, the seasons, her walks with the dog. Dad wrote to me every Sunday evening after church, always on an airmail flimsy, just a note about business and his customers.

He was always certain about his opinions, forming a view of things very quickly, and he hated bullying, over-zealous officialdom and hypocrisy. Years later he fell in love with his three year old grand-daughter when, she climbed on her chair at a performance of Punch and Judy, loudly berating Mr. Punch for his behaviour.

He hated waste and his three years as an Independent councillor on the Borough Council frequently provided good copy for the local newspaper, as he sought to keep ratepayers' money intact. He voted against expenditure on a Daimler for the Mayor, and, when another councillor pointed out that he may well benefit from the use of it at a future date, my father replied that he would attend Mayoral functions in his bread van.

Returning from abroad, I rang once to ask if he would look at the second hand car sales for me and he arranged for three vehicles to turn up on the Saturday. One potential vendor had to drive about 80 miles. When I queried this, he replied that it was a buyers' market. Some months later, prior to departing for the Far East, I asked him if he would see to the sale of the vehicle for me. The phone rang on the same day as the advert appeared and I heard him say – 'No, if you want to see it you must come here.' I reminded him of a statement earlier in the year and his reply was typical of his business head. It was, now, apparently, a sellers' market. He taught me the value of money.

One Friday my ship docked in Plymouth and I was given a long weekend leave pass. Using a dockside call box I asked the operator for a reverse charges call to my home number. I heard her speak to my father and say 'I have a Mr Todd calling from a Plymouth call box for you. Will you accept this as a reverse charge call?' And I heard him tell the operator, 'No!' And then he added 'Tell him he's a working man now earning a wage. So it's time he paid for his own calls.'

Whenever I returned on leave I saw little of him for he worked as hard as ever, and although my increasing maturity made our relationship better, my time at home was sometimes uncomfortable for it was obvious that their marriage was now something of a façade.

At the age of 59 Mum died and that was a shock, for we had become accustomed to the idea that she would outlive him. My first son was born on her birthday; five years later she passed away within half an hour of learning of the arrival of my younger boy. So she inextricably wove her romantic way not only into my life but also those of her two grandsons. The day after the funeral of her beloved younger sister, Mum developed jaundice that was soon confirmed as terminal cancer. Those final few months saw my parents draw closer than they had been for decades, my father even agreeing to both of them spending time with a faith healer. He promised Mum a campervan so that they could travel their own country together and she loved that idea.

After Mum's death he seemed lost, less assured, and spent his retirement heavily involved as a lay preacher with the church, and playing bowls. He looked forward to Saturdays when he prepared afternoon tea for his grandchildren, always baked beans on toast. Then two years after he was widowed he was admitted to hospital with a suspected internal cyst. The day after the exploratory operation he told me where to find his Will. 'Typical of Dad,' I thought, 'One little cyst and he thinks it's terminal.' Over the next several months I obstinately refuted the mounting evidence that his suspicions were correct. He came home, returned to hospital, came home again. He had modifications made to the house so he could sleep downstairs – that struck a chord somewhere. My sister moved in with him. He suffered a mild heart attack, but still I refused to think he might be terminally ill. Finally, in great pain, he was admitted once more for the surgeon to have 'another look'. It was the surgeon who met me when I visited that evening. He confirmed that the cancer was rampant and that it was 'a matter of weeks'. As I entered the room where my father lay I was formulating the cheerful, bright and positive statements an only son would make to his dying dad. But he cut me down, speechless.

'Don't say anything,' he said. "I know it's the end, and I am at ease with that now. I am refusing all food, as there is no point in wasting any more money on a dying man.' I stayed with him, but have no recollection of what we talked about. A few days later as I arrived for an evening visit, the nurse intercepted me and told me he had slipped into a coma.

I sat alongside him and saw for the first time an emaciated, husk of the man in whose shadow I had grown up, and wished that things had been different, that both he and Mum could have had a better relationship, and more time to enjoy their grandchildren, but his face was relaxed and he looked at peace as he breathed shallowly but regularly.

After an hour or so I left, when I should have stayed, for this man who had, according to my mother, lain awake most of the night after I was born during the war, worrying about the responsibility of bringing up a son, died alone in that single, joyless room before morning.

He had, true to character, refused all food in those last days because he said eating in his condition was a waste of food

I am almost at the age he died at now and am still gaining a better perspective of each of my parents and their relationship. Divorced and retired, I spend six months of the year sailing on my own around the West and North of Scotland, sometimes imagining how my mother would love the experiences; meeting the people and visiting the places that are a part of me. My yacht is named romantically in her memory. Yet nowadays, it is my father who more often dominates my thoughts, for I frequently imagine him close by in the role of mentor, his sheer practicality and pragmatism helping me manage situations that threaten to overwhelm me at times, whereas my mother's romanticism would have me shipwrecked on some deserted white beach:

As Tennyson wrote:

Yet all experience is an arch wherethro'
Gleams that untravell'd world, whose margin fades
For ever and for ever when I move.
How dull it is to pause, to make an end,
To rust unburnish'd, not to shine in use!

My mother's dreams of that gleaming, untravell'd world, those hundreds of Timbuktu's waiting to be explored, were always at odds with those of a business man whose own dream of a life dedicated to the church was thwarted by not being the eldest son, and who then submersed himself in the responsibilities of family and work. 'God bless,' he'd say. God bless indeed.

Those were the Notes C. C. B. B A.A

On a sunny Saturday I had walked the short distance from the Royal Marine Barracks and turned into Union Street, the long thoroughfare that led into the centre of Plymouth. I had left the comfort of my room with no intention of buying anything apart from a newspaper, a cup of coffee and a scone. The pavement was slightly obstructed in one place where a used car dealer had parked a couple of vehicles on an expanse of concrete between two buildings.

I stopped and looked at the nearest one. It had a big cardboard sign on the windscreen advising it for sale at £25! I had never seen a car advertised at such a low price. Suddenly the idea of owning a vehicle, and enjoying the independence that a set of wheels promised, was very attractive.

I walked around it. Within a few minutes the car salesman was standing alongside me. "It's a good little runner; in good order throughout, and taxed for the remainder of the year, That's worth the £25!"

"Can you take me for a quick test drive?" I asked. He removed the 'for sale' sign, and then returned from his little porta-cabin with the key. Within fifteen minutes we returned and he parked back on the concrete standing.

"So what do you think?" he asked.

It's not got a radio I observed as I glanced at the dashboard

"These old Morris Minors predate car-radios. But they do have a place for a radio." He said.

I looked at the dashboard again, but could see nowhere for a radio, and said so.

"Most people use the parcel shelf for a transistor radio."

"A what sort of shelf? " I asked, and he pointed out the small flat shelf behind the rear seat just below the rear window.

"A parcel shelf?" I queried, the only things I have ever seen on that shelf in other cars have been boxes of paper tissues."

I agreed to buy it, and said I would have to return to the barracks to get my Post Office Savings book so I could get the cash. I made my way back up Union Street. This took me past the local pawnshop. I gazed through the glass plate window and it was the blue, transistor radio that caught my eye immediately. The front of it was a chromed grill that concealed the speakers. It was about the size of an A4 sheet of paper, and just 4 inches deep, All in all it was a triumph of design and construction. Years later I learned that this elegant model won an award from the Design Council.

This seemed truly appropriate and apt for I listened to some of the most outstanding music of the 60s on it. Years later it became a fixture on the window ledge in the garage where, like my dreams and memories, it ended up gathering dust and cobwebs.

On that spring day the radio cost me almost a third of what I had paid for the car but I was delighted as it would be a welcome addition to my room in the barracks. When I got the keys of the vehicle the first thing I did was to put the radio on the parcel shelf.

The following weekend I drove home to Wales. and the radio kept me company. During that summer I made that journey several times. I spent most of those weekends with my girlfriend Mari, who was completing her teacher training at the college in my hometown.

One warm Saturday morning we sat on the springy green grass overlooking the sea. Mari stretched out her arms and said "Isn't this perfect? On days like this, on soft cushiony turf like this, I always feel like doing handstands and somersaults". She was lovely, so natural and full of the joys of life but it had to come to an end. Mari would be moving away to begin teaching probably in the London area, whilst I was about to start specialised mountaineering and climbing courses.

As we talked these things over, it became obvious that Mari was seeking some sort of commitment from me, and that was something I was unwilling to make. We talked for hours. At one point in our discussion I said that we could continue our relationship on a sort of ad hoc basis. I said I would visit her when I was able to get away from my Royal Marine commitments, but this did not go down well with Mari. It gradually dawned on me that I was in danger of destroying and losing the best thing that had ever happened to me, so at one stage I put my arms around her and said "Oh, Mari, wait for me please?

She pulled away, and said with feeling "You seem to want the penny and the bun." And it was true. That final weekend we drove miles together, and, all the time the radio played away on the parcel shelf. It always seemed to be the same tune. It was sung by a Welsh girl from Swansea. Her voice filled the tune and words with *Hiraeth* that lovely Welsh word that implies homesickness, love, emotion and nostalgia. It was a musical poem imbued with longing. It was difficult to contemplate the coming months without seeing Mari, and I only had to hear this tune to be reminded of her.

Within a few months she and a few of her friends had successfully applied for jobs in London. They rented a house together, and got on with their lives. Within the year I learned that Mari had started dating an Australian man and that marriage was being contemplated

I continued to drive back and forth to Wales whenever I had the chance to do so, and the radio played on the parcel shelf. During one visit home my mother asked me about Mari. Mari had often come to my home with me, and had even called in to see my mother when I wasn't there. I told my mother that we had split up and it was obviously a disappointment to her. She proceeded to sing Mari's praises, and to tell me I was a fool.

Unknown to me my mother had got into the habit of submitting all the girls I took home to a vanity check. As you walked through the front door of the house and entered the narrow hall, the stairs were immediately to the left. Between the stairs and the door to the kitchen there was a short length of wall, and on this wall there was a large oval mirror. My mother had noticed that many of my girlfriends that walked along the hall to enter the living room, failed to resist the temptation to look at themselves in the mirror. She took great pleasure in telling me that Mari had never done so.

When I returned to Plymouth, I found a letter awaiting me, telling me that Mari was engaged. She was intending to move to Australia. I decided to write to Mari and congratulate her. Even as I wrote the letter I knew I had lost the girl who would have been the making of me. I closed the letter with a short poem that I had written.

'You can't have your cake
And eat it'
She spelt it out in white and black,
Defiant almost, as she said it.
Go now, Right Now,
And don't look back
For Love can't square a circle
A truth she'd always known
But he'd blindly chosen not to see it
And so he reaped what he had sown.

Within the year I was posted to Singapore, where I continued to live out my dream of living an exciting life. Several months after arriving there a huge Military training exercise involving thousands of men saw us sailing across to northern Australia. It took place in the huge area of Northern Territory. The exercise lasted a week and we were relieved when it drew to a close one Friday, and we learned that we were to be 'bussed' hundreds of miles south to the Brisbane coast for some rest and recreational leave.

It was dark by the time we had all boarded the coaches, and we moved off along miles of narrow unlit single tracked road. It was not long before all the tired Marines had fallen asleep, and we all slept through the night. I finally stirred as the morning light slanted through the windows of the coach and the sun's rays washed over the Australian landscape, the driver sensed that his passengers were waking up and turned on the coach radio. The coach was suddenly filled with the voice of that young Swansea girl, the words still full of Hireath and nostalgia.

1 thought of Mari and how she had chosen to settle out here. Within seconds, prompted by tiredness and homesickness everyone in the coach was humming the tune, or singing along with her. My eyes filled with tears as the poetry of the words transported me back to a love I'd lost. Those were indeed the days my Mari.

The Power, and Knock-on Effect of Good Feedback

The mobile phone vibrated in my shirt pocket. This signal made me think it was an electric stimulus for my heart. In a way it was, for the incoming call gave me a real lift. I managed to retrieve the phone and press the green button before the signal failed. It was a call from my friend Terry. It was always good to hear her voice. She had some feedback for me. A couple of days previously she had met up with a friend, Jan, who had expressed an interest in reading anything that I had written. Terry had asked me if I had any preference as to what she would give her. So I said that the best thing to do would be to take along anything that had given Terry pleasure.

Just two days later the friend had rung Terry to tell her how much she had enjoyed both the stories that told of some of our sailing experiences. I was shopping in the Inverness 'Pound-Stretcher' shop when I took the call, and as Terry told how the stories had made Jan laugh. I could tell from Terry's voice how much enjoyment she had got from the conversation, and how she was enjoying passing the feedback on to me. I was obstructing the aisle, so we closed the line and agreed to talk that evening.

I decided to treat myself to a coffee in Marks and Spencer. I'd never been in that cafeteria before. I had a brief conversation with the woman in the queue behind me and made her smile at my inability to master the routine of tray, plate, tongs and scone and butter. I made a point of thanking her for her help. The restaurant was full of 'regulars' enjoying their weekly treat of an M &S lunch of soup and cheese toasties. I sat at a very small table. I ate and drank quickly as the good feeling inspired by the feedback had reminded me of an uncompleted idea.

I put my plate, cup and saucer on my tray. I glanced at the table alongside that was of a similar size. The old lady sitting there was struggling to manage her large plate on the small table. She had finished her coffee so I offered to take the empty cup to give her more space. She was profuse with her thanks and gave me a nice smile. I carried the tray across to where one of the staff was processing all the used crockery. Yet again I was favoured with a 'thank you' and a smile.

I made my way through the Men's clothing section where a few old men were gossiping and obstructing the aisle and I resisted the temptation to push through them and call them old fishwives. I stepped out into the pedestrianised main street. The air was full of music. Everything seemed beautiful. In front of the Royal Bank an old man sat on his coat and strummed and plucked sweet notes from the strings of his guitar. The notes rose above him and the breeze that blew all the way from the cold waters of Loch Ness into the Great Glen, tumbling them throughout the concourses, where they fell like audio confetti on the pedestrians. I dropped a coin into his guitar case and told him how sweet his music sounded.

Three weeks previously I had lost my small coin purse. I noticed its absence from my pocket when I was in one of the well-stocked charity shops. I'd been in there about ten minutes before a book title almost hit me between the eyes. I knew I had to buy it, for it reminded me of Terry. At almost £3.00, combined with the price of a padded envelope and the postage it would be a reasonable Valentine's day's gift. I took it to the cash desk reached for my purse, for I knew there was a £5 note in it, but the purse was gone.

Upset at losing almost £7.00 I told myself that I would not spend any more money in town that day, and that, by not buying the book, I was also saving money. Every week that I went to town, I would visit the charity shop. The book was still there but the hurt at losing my purse and the money in it was still strong.

Now three weeks later I saw the book 'Rebecca' on the shelf again. It was alongside one of my favourite love stories, 'Pastoral' by Nevil Shute. I read the last few pages of 'Pastoral' and felt the emotions well up as my eyes watered. Surely a sign! But after the phone call I knew that today had to be the day that, no matter what it cost, the book had to be posted to Terry. So, lots of people and businesses benefited from the wonderful feedback, but none more than me! The bubble of love inside me, like all bubbles was surrounded by a rainbow.